CW00922606

BIRDS OF RYE HARBOUR

A Birdwatching Logbook

Birdwatching Tips

The aim of this logbook is to encourage you to look out for birds along this stretch of coastline, and record when and where you see them.

It is important to get to know how a bird moves, flies, and sings as well as identifying the shape, so the illustrations are there to show you important features to look out for, and the accompanying text tells you how the bird behaves.

Becoming familiar with common birds allows you to spot rarer sightings, so this book will introduce you to the great variety of birds living in and around Rye Harbour.

Tadorna tadorna

Body length: *55-65cm*

Where to spot:

Lakes and lagoons, grassy

areas

All Year

SHELDUCK

Shelducks have beautiful and striking plumage, making them a distinctive spot either on the ponds and lagoons, or grazing on the vegetated areas. They eat mainly worms and molluscs so are often seen alone or in small groups looking for food in the shallows.

Males have a bulbous protuberance at the top of the beak distinguishing them from females, and are slightly bigger but apart from that, they look the same. Shelducklings are adorable little black-and-white striped fluffballs.

They have a high-pitched, hissy quack.

Date	Notes

CURLEW

Numenius arquata

Body length: *48-57cm*

Where to spot:

Mudflats, saltmarsh,

shallow lagoons

All Year

A Curlew's long curved beak - up to 15cm on females and 10cm on males and youngsters - has an orangey base and makes this large wader easy to see as it pokes and prods in the mud for worms and shellfish. They have a reddish tinge to their plumage with diamond patterns on the wings. The Whimbrel is similar but smaller, greyer, and has a distinctly stripy head.

The call of a Curlew across the landscape is evocative and insistent, and says their name: "cour-lee".

Date	Notes

Recurvirostra avosetta

Body length: *42-46cm*

Where to spot:

Tidal flats, shallow ponds,

muddy pools

All Year

These pied waders with their upturned beaks and delicate form are a treat to see, and have enjoyed an increase in number due to conservation and protection efforts. They sweep that specialised beak back and forth in the water to sift tiny aquatic invertebrates, but they also swim in deep pools, up-ending like ducks.

The juveniles have shorter, straighter beaks and more mottled colouration.

They have a piping "kwip-kwip-kwip" call.

Date	Notes

OYSTERCATCHER

Haematopus ostralegus

Body length: *39-44cm*

Where to spot:

Open marsh, tidal

lagoons, beaches

All Year

Oystercatchers are large waders, making their presence known with both their confidence and their call. They are bold and noisy, gathering in groups to nest on bare, pebbly ground. Unmistakable colouring, with black upperparts and white belly, and pink legs. They use their long, bright orange beak for hammering or prising open cockles and mussels.

The two main Oystercatcher calls are a high-pitched "keep keep keeep" in flight as well as a more trilling "ki-ki-ki-ki" when huddled in groups.

Date	Notes

Tringa totanus

Body length: *24-27cm*

Where to spot:

Coastal grassland, shallow

ponds, marshy areas

All Year

You may not be close enough to notice the red legs and black-tipped beak but the Redshank is frequently seen rootling in mud and wet soil to find worms, insect larvae and crustaceans. Juveniles have orangey-yellow legs and a paler beak.

Redshanks often hang out with other waders in a mixed flock so learning the shape, size and habit of one species helps to make it clear who's who.

Calls are a pleasantly musical "tyoo tyooee", often heard as the birds take flight.

Date	Notes

SKYLARK

Alauda arvensis

Body length: *16-18cm*

Where to spot:

High above vegetated

areas, fenceposts

All Year

Despite a rather nondescript appearance, the Skylark is one of our most accomplished singers, showing its fitness and vigour to predators, potential mates and rivals by performing its song while flying upwards with fluttering wings.

Streaks of black in the ochre and tawny plumage give the bird a mottled look.

A Skylark's song is a marathon of trills, whistles, chirrups and mimicry, lasting up to 15 minutes, and from a height of 100 metres or more.

Date	Notes

Egretta garzetta

Body length: *55-65cm*

Where to spot:

Shallow pools, sluices,

sheltered ponds

All Year

LITTLE EGRET

Little Egrets are elegant and stylish, and stand motionless in the water or on the bank waiting for their moment to strike out and catch a fish. Long black legs and beak complete the look; the yellow feet are not often seen in the murky shallows.

Like a small white Heron in flight, they pull up their neck into their body and trail their legs out behind.

They are mostly silent but sometimes squawk on take off.

Date	Notes

GREYLAG GOOSE

Anser anser

Body length: *74-84cm*

Where to spot:

Lagoons, lakes, grassy

areas

All Year

These large birds are the ancestors of our domestic geese, except they are still powerful flyers unlike our farmyard poultry. They graze on vegetation and build their nests on the sides of pools and lagoons where they can introduce the goslings to water. Numbers of Greylags swell in winter as geese from other parts of Europe join our resident population.

The call is what you would expect from a goose: a nasally squeaky honk.

Date	Notes

Chroicocephalus ridibundus

Body length: *35-39cm*

Where to spot:

Sandbanks, shingle,

shallow pools and sea

All Year

BLACK-HEADED GULL

Black-headed Gulls are finely built with attractive plumage and pretty faces, with a slightly lazy flight as they look down for morsels of food. They nest and roost colonially, and are bold and raucous so it's easy to work out where they are.

In winter the black (or rather, dark chocolate brown) head reduces to a dot behind the eye. Juveniles are beautifully patterned, with a mosaic of ochre, black and grey.

A loud "kreeyaarr! kreeyaarrrr!" is the main scolding call, with shorter sharper notes at times.

Date	Notes

Use this page as a quick ticklist

Date completed:

RINGED PLOVER

Charadrius hiaticula

Body length: *17-19cm*

Where to spot:

Shoreline, muddy flats,

shallow pools

All Year

These little plovers have distinctive markings and scurry along the shoreline and mudflats looking for invertebrates and tiny molluscs. The white belly, grey-brown back and black eyemask and collar contrasts with the relatively short orange legs.

Their flight is fast with clipped wingbeats, and white traces on the wings are similar to many other waders, so look for the facial markings to determine whether it's a ringed plover.

Calls are varied but are mostly two-syllable: "doo-eep".

Date	Notes

Fulica atra

Body length: *36-42cm*

Where to spot:

Vegetated pools and

lakes, reedbeds

All Year

Coots like reedy ponds to nest and feed, and they are fiercely territorial, driving away intruders, unafraid to get involved in fights and tussles with other coots.

The white beak and frontal plate against the black body makes this waterbird easy to spot, and the juveniles are a grey version of their parents. They run across the water to take flight, showing off their lobed feet.

Calls vary from a repeated "kark" to a more trumpeting "pe-oo", as well a short sharp "pitt! pitt!".

Date	Notes

MARSH HARRIER

Circus aeruginosus

Body length: *43-55cm*

Where to spot:

Over marshland and

reedbeds

All Year

Marsh Harriers are our largest harrier, nesting in reedbeds and hunting small mammals and birds over marshy areas. They hold their wings in a shallow 'v' with primary wing feathers splayed. The black wing tips are more pronounced on the smaller male; the creamy head more obvious on the female.

They perform spectacular tumbling display flights, with pairs occasionally locking talons.

The call is quite squeaky and high-pitched for such an impressive raptor.

Date	Notes

Oenanthe oenanthe

Body length: *14-16cm*

Where to spot:

Scrubby undergrowth,

fenceposts

Summer

WHEATEAR

Wheatears are slightly larger than a Robin, and have an upright stance typical of many thrushes. They often perch on fenceposts and atop brambles, their black eyemask being an obvious feature against the pale grey back and buff-coloured breast.

They spend the winter in Africa, so are seen both breeding and on passage along the coast.

They have a slightly scratchy crackly song, as well as a sharp "chack" for contact or alarm.

Date	Notes

STOCK DOVE

Columba oenas

Body length: *28-32cm*

Where to spot:

Vegetated areas, flying

fast overhead

All Year

Although easily mistaken for a Wood or Feral Pigeon, these beautifully understated doves lack the white wing markings of their pigeon cousins, and have a dark eye giving them a soft, gentle look.

They mainly eat seeds, so are seen flying between scrubby areas, and they are smaller and more compact than wood pigeons.

The call is like a monosyllabic version of a wood pigeon call: "hoo...hooo...hoo...hoo...".

Date	Notes

Arenaria interpres

Body length: *21-24cm*

Where to spot:

Shoreline, pebbly weedy

pools and mudflats

All Year

TURNSTONE

These busy little waders, as the name suggests, search for food by turning stones, pebbles and seaweed over with their beaks to tweeze small morsels of invertebrate food that are lurking underneath.

Many waders change their plumage entirely between winter and summer, and Turnstones are no exception, donning a bright, ochre-umber-orange outfit for summer and a more muted, brown and black for winter. The black neck and chin markings remain throughout.

The call is a whirring chuckle.

Date	Notes

CORMORANT

Phalacrocorax carbo

Body length: *77-94cm*

Where to spot:

Sandbanks, pools and

lagoons

All Year

Most birds - especially aquatic species - apply oil from their preen gland to their feathers to keep them waterproof, but Cormorants are diving birds so have plumage which purposely absorbs water to allow for effective fishing. Consequently they are often seen standing on rocks and sandbanks with their wings 'hanging out to dry' in the sun and breeze. Large, dark, and reptilian, cormorants can look quite prehistoric.

Unremarkable gurgling calls are mainly heard at the colony.

Date	Notes

Vanellus vanellus

Body length: *28-31cm*

Where to spot:

Seashore, grassy areas,

lakes and lagoons

All Year

LAPWING

One of our prettiest plovers, Lapwings have a long crest, and iridescent plumage with a white belly and cheeks. They are about the size of a Pigeon, and often flock in large numbers, especially in winter.

Like many waders the nest is a simple scrape, and the chicks are up and out only hours after they have hatched, following their parents to feed on tiny worms and insects.

The tumbling displays of the males with their rounded, black-and-white wings are accompanied by a distinctive and upbeat song: "wee-oo-ipp choo-ipp wee-iddle-ipp".

Date	Notes

TUFTED DUCK

Aythya fuligula

Body length: *40-47cm*

Where to spot:

Vegetated pools and

lagoons

All year

Both males and females sport a tuft, although the male is a deep, glossy, inky blue-black with a white side, and the female a rich brown all over. They feed and breed on lakes and pools with good cover as this provides them with the plants and insects that they eat.

They are diving ducks so frequently disappear to feed before surfacing again - sometimes a surprising distance away.

The female's call is a rolling "prrrrrr prrrrr prrr", and the male's call is more bubbly.

Date	Notes

Sterna hirundo

Body length: *34-37cm*

Where to spot:

Pebbly shores, fishing

over ponds and lakes

Summer

COMMON TERN

These dainty seabirds are migratory marvels, wintering in Africa and returning to our coastline to breed. Their pale grey and white plumage with dark tail streamers give them a unique outline compared to gulls, and a bobbing, dancing flight pattern shows how comfortable they are on the wing.

They can be noisy as they defend their eggs and chicks in the scrape of a nest from predators by dive-bombing and yelling. The main call is a "dee-oo-wee dee-oo-wee".

Date	Notes

BLACKBIRD

Turdus merula

Body length: *23-29cm*

Where to spot:

Scrubby undergrowth,

gardens, mature trees

All Year

One of our favourite garden birds, the yellow beak and eye ring of the male can be seen clearly as they frequently stop, look up, and then carry on hunting for worms. They hop and run, and fly low to the ground between shrubs, trees and favourite perches.

Females are a blend of beautiful chocolate browns, and young Blackbirds are really quite spotty.

The males often sing their delightful melodies in the evening from trees and lamp posts. Alarm calls are sharp "plinks" or a flurry of indignant notes.

Date	Notes

Sturnus vulgaris

Body length: *19-22cm*

Where to spot:

Reedbeds, scrub, lawns,

telegraph wires

All Year

STARLING

Accomplished formation flyers, Starlings are often seen in groups zipping over the vegetation, triangular wings beating fast as they change direction: this manoeuvring is to outwit aerial predators.

Noisy and gregarious, Starlings gather in family groups; the juveniles with their grey-brown plumage are easy to spot among the glossy adults. They eat lawn grubs and insects but will also visit fruit trees to pick at fallen apples.

The song is a rich medley of clicking, buzzing, whistling and mimicry.

Date	Notes

SHOVELER

Anas clypeata

Body length: *44-52cm*

Where to spot:

Open water and marsh

with vegetation

All Year

This duck may look like the more familiar Mallard, but that big shovelly beak is a giveaway, even at a distance. They have a lot of white on them, and a dark brown belly; the females share the cryptic plumage of many ducks so the beak is the best clue.

The wide spatulate beak is used to sift plant matter and tiny insects from the surface of calm pools and ponds - a technique shared by the avocet. They tend to stay in pairs or small groups.

The call is a nasal, hooting "kook kook".

Date	Notes

More birds you may see:

GREAT CRESTED GREBE

KINGFISHER

HERRING GULL

SAND MARTIN

LINNET

*You will find
these in the
other books
in the series*

Notes & Sketches

Notes & Sketches

Index